General Care and Maintenance of
Popular Tortoises

Philippe de Vosjoli

April 27/04

The Herpetocultural Library

Advanced Vivarium Systems, Inc.
P.O. Box 6050, Mission Viejo, CA 92690

Library of Congress Catalog Card Number: 96-183295.

ISBN #1-882770-37-4

Printed in Singapore

Cover photography by Jim Bridges and Bob Prince.
Graphic design and layout by Michelle Florance.

Contents

ACKNOWLEDGEMENTS

The author would like to thank Chris Estep of Reptile Haven, Chuck Henderson of Rancho Tortuga, Mike and Margaret Hawley, Micki and Brad Dutenhoeffer, and Chris Wood for their help in providing photographs.

Introduction

Tortoises are among the most endangered families of reptiles. Surely the day will come when all wild populations of tortoises will be protected, but there is little guarantee that this will be enough to assure their survival. Destruction of their habitat, exploitation of them as a food source, and collection of them for the pet trade all contribute to the decline of these animals, as do unsound wildlife laws.

It is not clear why there has not been more public protest (including by turtle and tortoise clubs) against these laws. As an example, the United States Endangered Species Act covering **non-native** amphibian and reptile species, and therefore restricting (through red tape) interstate traffic of **non-native** reptile species in this country, helps no one, neither the animals nor the herpetoculturist. Basically, this law discourages people from keeping or breeding endangered species and requires paperwork to monitor the movement of these species in the United States. At least in the case of the Indian python and the Bengal monitor, it has resulted in a decline of these species in the United States and has hindered efforts of captive-breeding. In the case of Galapagos or radiated tortoises, regulating commercial traffic within the United States does absolutely nothing in terms of the status of wild populations and promotes essentially useless red tape.

Another unsound law is the one stating that only turtles of at least four inches in length can be sold commercially in the United States. This law was put in place because children contracted salmonellosis from baby turtles, mostly red-eared sliders. One consequence of this law is that it places collecting pressure on

1

animals of reproductive age—in the case of smaller tortoises, the small percentage that have managed to grow to reproductive size. This law discourages captive breeding, field culture, management, and sustained harvesting of wild tortoises. Adult tortoises should be protected through appropriate legislation in the countries of origin. On the other hand, captive hatched and/or bred animals should be legal to sell in the pet trade, with a certain percentage of the tortoises kept aside and raised for restocking or for breeding stock. At the very least within the United States, tortoises should be exempt from the "four-inch turtle law." As for salmonellosis, turtles simply should not be sold to minors without parental consent to assume responsibility for their care, and adults should be informed via a release form of the potential danger of salmonellosis. Turtles are not living toys and should not be treated as such. If there is to be a future availability of tortoises for keeping in captivity, these issues must be addressed, and quickly.

At this point in time, it is important to realize that owning tortoises is a privilege, one which is likely to be short-lived. Prospective tortoise owners should make every effort to keep their animals under optimal conditions and to strive to breed them in captivity. Tortoises are not children's playthings or cheap living toys that you put in your yard and then ignore. If, however, the sight of a tortoise is something that generates amazement in you, and if the prospect of owning, observing and interacting with tortoises on a daily basis is something that you think would add greatly to your experience of life, then you are probably correct in deciding to own these animals.

This book covers the basic care of the most popular and commonly imported tortoises. For the most part it does not cover breeding or veterinary medicine. This book focuses on basic husbandry. For more detailed information look for *The Tortoise Manual* I am coauthoring with Sean McKeown, herpetologist and a curator of reptiles and amphibians in different zoos in the United States for over 20 years. It covers subjects such as breeding and incubation of eggs, and it includes more detailed health information. See also the excellent books by Andy Highfield and others in the Reference section.

2

Selection

Climate requirements

At the present time, tortoises are being imported from temperate climates such as Europe and Russia, from semiarid regions such as East Africa, and from humid tropical climates such as Southeast Asia and West Africa. One primary consideration when selecting a tortoise is whether you will be able to provide the conditions required for its optimum care, and to a significant degree it will depend on the climate in which you live. In several regions of the United States, you can keep various tortoise species outdoors during part of the year. For example, red-footed tortoises, yellow-footed tortoises, and elongated tortoises can be successfully kept and bred outdoors in south Florida with relatively little investment in their facilities. African spurred and leopard tortoises are successfully kept and bred outdoors year-round in southern California and Arizona, as long as heated shelters are available to them during the cold and wet days of winter. Temperate-climate tortoises must be cooled down in the winter if they are to breed and live long. If you live in an area with cool winters it will be easier to provide this requirement. The ease with which you can provide facilities and the possibility of keeping the animals outdoors during at least part of the year should definitely be among your considerations when selecting a tortoise.

If you cannot keep tortoises outdoors, then you must simulate the essential features of their environment indoors. Doing this requires space as well as landscaping, artificial lights, heating systems, and, in some cases, cooling systems.

Size

All tortoises require a fair amount of space in order to thrive, so choosing the appropriate size species is a critical factor in selecting a tortoise. One of the hardiest and most readily available is the African spurred tortoise *(Geochelone sulcata)*, which is now bred by the thousands in the United States. These tortoises have a lot going for them, including looks and personality, but they grow quickly and they grow large. Adults require an enclosure equivalent to a room measuring twelve feet by twelve feet, and a larger enclosure is preferable. Although they don't grow quite as quickly, leopard tortoises *(Geochelone pardalis)* will also require the equivalent of a large portion of a room—at least an eight-foot by eight-foot enclosure—as adults. Anything smaller is inhumane and could threaten the health and long-term survival of these tortoises. Small species such as pancake tortoises, star tortoises, Egyptian tortoises, and the European tortoises are better choices if your space is limited.

Hardiness

Some tortoises are more difficult to keep than others. For example, star tortoises *(Geochelone elegans)* and forest hingeback tortoises *(Kinixys erosa)* are best left to experienced tortoise keepers. On the other hand, Russian tortoises, captive-bred European tortoises, African spurred tortoises, and leopard tortoises are generally good choices for beginners. In warm regions such as south Florida, red-footed tortoises are also a good choice.

Red-footed tortoise (Geochelone carbonaria). This large tortoise is very attractive, personable and reasonably hardy if heat and at least 70% relative humidity are provided.

Wild-caught versus captive-bred tortoises

As a rule, captive-bred tortoises are a better bet than wild-caught animals. They are less likely to be parasitized or diseased. You will also know their age and something about their background. Captive-raised tortoises will also tend to breed more readily than wild-caught animals who may take several years to establish and cycle into a reproductive pattern. If there is one drawback to captive-bred animals, it is that hatchlings of several species can prove delicate and require optimal conditions for rearing in captivity. In most cases, it will be worthwhile for the beginning tortoise keeper to pay extra for purchasing captive-bred animals that are older and larger, usually at least 6 months to a year old. On the other hand, meticulous attention to providing the proper conditions and diet will allow most herpetoculturists to success-fully raise baby tortoises.

For experienced keepers, wild-caught tortoises can provide an increased and more diversified genetic pool for captive-breeding. However, experience is generally required to deparasitize and establish wild-caught tortoises. Because all tortoise species are threatened, there should be concerted efforts to reduce commercial exploitation of adult wild-caught tortoises and to develop herpetocultural systems for captive-propagation.

Personality

Some tortoises are so beautiful that their good looks make up for their relatively unresponsive personalities. But as any experienced tortoise keeper will inform you, tortoises have varying personalities: some are shyer than others, some are more outgoing, some are more aggressive, others are more aloof. And every once in a while you may find an exceptional animal that surprises you with its responsiveness and intelligence. Nonetheless, some generalizations can be made.

Top ranking in terms of personality are some commonly available and not-too-expensive species. Greek tortoises and Russian tortoises tend to be very personable. They are alert and will rush to get food; they will eventually eat out of your hands and climb on your shoes to beg. Red-footed tortoises have pleasant outgoing personalities—among the best, if that is what you are seeking. African spurred tortoises are intelligent and personable, to a

5

degree, but they commonly remain somewhat wary; occasional individuals, however, are great personable animals. Leopard tortoises are moderately personable, but as a whole this species is relatively indifferent to its human owners. For having interacting personalities, hinge-back tortoises don't rank very high either. On the other hand, Burmese brown tortoises usually do. Galapagos tortoises actually like to be petted and rank high among the most personable tortoises. Aldabras, however, are not nearly as friendly and have been described as dull.

Of course, there are always exceptions to any rule. It is true that to a degree you will reap what you sow. Obtain a baby tortoise and encourage interaction, regularly attempting gentle physical contact such as petting its head or neck area, hand-feed it on occasion, and you will provide an environment for the more interactive and extroverted side of your tortoise's personality to emerge.

Health
Once you have selected a species that you think you will be able to accommodate, the next step is to select a potentially healthy specimen.

Generally, a captive-bred animal from an established breeder is one of your best choices for a tortoise pet. Captive-bred animals

A simple setup for pancake tortoises. Basking lights and high UVB reptile fluorescent bulbs are provided. The author also recommends shelters, cork bark or stacked flattened rocks for this species. Food is also best offered on paper plates to reduce the probability of sand impaction when feeding.

6

are less likely to have parasites and more likely to be healthy. And an experienced breeder will be able to provide first-hand information on successfully raising the species in question. Captive-bred tortoises are commonly available through specialized reptile stores, breeders, and reptile shows. Periodicals such as *The Vivarium, Reptiles,* and *Reptile and Amphibian Magazine* contain advertising that can help you find tortoise breeders. Turtle and tortoise societies are also good sources of information. Whenever possible it is best to buy an animal that you are able to examine before purchasing, rather than obtaining one sight unseen by mail order; however, there are now many reputable reptile dealers who will provide you with honest information over the telephone.

Longevity

Tortoises rank among the longest lived land vertebrates. There is a record of 127 years for a greek tortoise (*Testudo graeca*). The large tortoises Galapagos (*Geochelone elephantopus*) and Aldabras (*Geochelone gigantea*) can exceed 60 years. There is a 25 year record for the pancake tortoise and 30 year record for the leopard tortoise. Red-footed tortoises can exceed 20 years as can hinge-back tortoises. In short, tortoises have the potential for long lives.

If flattened rocks are provided, pancake tortoises will entertain you with their rock climbing abilities.

Guidelines for Selecting
Potentially Healthy Animals

At the outset, careful attention to selection will increase significantly your chances of purchasing a potentially healthy animal. Whether your prospective tortoise is captive-bred or wild-caught, use the following criteria for selection:

1. If the tortoise is awake, it should appear wide-eyed. Half-opened, swollen and watery eyes are signs of possible illness. A tortoise that is active or observed feeding is a good potential selection. The eyes must not appear sunken, and the cheeks must appear rounded, with no visible outline of the cheekbones. The nostrils must be clear and free of mucus. Using a thumb, gently press up against the throat of a tortoise if possible. If mucus emerges from the nostrils, then the tortoise may have a respiratory infection. Gaping and forced exhalations are common symptoms of pneumonia.

2. Ask that the tortoise be handed to you. A healthy tortoise should give the impression of good weight for its size. If you are surprised by how light the tortoise seems, this may be a sign of disease. A healthy tortoise demonstrates muscular vigor. A strong response of withdrawal into the shell is a good sign. If you gently pull on a hind leg and get a strong withdrawal response, this is an indication of potentially good health. Avoid animals that give the impression of being limp.

3. Closely examine the shell top (carapace) and bottom (plastron) for signs of injury or bleeding beneath the epithelial (surface)

layer. Do not purchase animals with sub-epithelial shell bleeding. Look for any swelling of individual limbs. Examine the eyes and the sides of the head. Look for swelling of the cheek areas. If you look at the head from above, it should appear bilaterally symmetrical.

4. Check the edges of the beak of the tortoise, looking for breaks, swelling, or caseous material; avoid animals with these symptoms.

5. Examine the vent area (the opening to the cloaca at the base of the tail). It should be flush with the base of the tail, not swollen or crusty. The presence of watery fecal smears around the vent is a sign of parasitism and/or enteritis. Check the fecal matter in the tortoise's enclosure if it is present. Watery feces are typical signs of parasitism and gastroenteritis. Large amounts of urates (white chalky in appearance) can be a sign of kidney disease. Keep in mind, however, that newly imported animals may have watery feces at first; with proper care, the feces should firm up. If a turtle appears otherwise healthy but has watery feces, realize that it will have to be checked and treated for parasites. Healthy tortoises have soft, formed and often fibrous feces.

Remember: a healthy tortoise will have good weight, muscular vigor, a clean and uninjured shell, a bilaterally symmetrical head, clear and wide-open eyes when awake, slightly rounded cheeks (but not unusually swollen cheeks or asymmetrically swollen cheeks), limbs that are neither swollen nor injured, good withdrawal response when a hind limb is gently pulled, and a vent that is flush with the base of the tail, without smears of watery feces.

TERMINOLOGY

Carapace:	Dorsal (back) part of the shell.
Plastron:	Ventral (belly) part of the shell.
Cloaca:	The common chamber into which the genital, urinary and digestive canals empty their contents.

Sexing

As a general rule, adult male tortoises of several species (not all) have a concave plastron (lower shell), whereas females have a flattened plastron. There are several exceptions, including pancake tortoises *(Malacochersus tornieri)* and Russian tortoises *(Testudo horsfieldii)*. The most reliable indicator of sex in most species is the length of the tail and the distance of the vent from the body. Generally, males have the vent opening at a greater distance from the body than do females. The tail of the males of most species will also be longer and thicker than that of females; however, it is not obvious in all species. Another method used to sex tortoises is to observe the angle formed by the anal scutes just anterior to the vent or base of the tail area. In males the anal scute angle will usually be wider than in females. This method often can be used to sex immature tortoises.

Close-up of ram-like gular process on male spurred tortoise. Photo by Chris Estep.

Underside of male (left) versus female (right) Russian tortoise. Note in this species the significantly longer tail and the wider anal scute angle of the male. In this species, males do not have a concave plastron and are typically smaller than females.

Male tortoises are usually smaller than females, but there are many exceptions such as African spurred tortoises. In general, hatchling tortoises are difficult to sex, but you can make an educated guess by comparing tail width, vent distance from the body, and the anal scute angle.

In tortoises, sex is temperature determined and eggs incubated at the lower range of incubation temperatures result in a high percentage of males while eggs incubated at the higher range result in high numbers of females. This is the reverse of what we find in lizards such as geckos where low temperatures result in high numbers of females and high temperatures yield high numbers of males.

Plastra of leopard tortoises. The male, on the left has longer and thicker tail, broader anal scute angle and slightly concave posterior plastron. The female with smaller tail, smaller anal scute angle and flat plastron is on the right. Photo by Chris Estep.

11

Number of Tortoises per Group

Because female tortoises generally are not particularly aggressive, you can usually keep them together. Males, on the other hand, are usually combative and territorial, at least during the breeding season. With most species you can keep several pairs together, but with other species you can do so only inside a very large enclosure. African spurred tortoise males, for example, tend to be very territorial and aggressive and males must be kept singly. During combat the male's usual objective is to flip the opposing male on his back. Subdominant animals may be stressed, injured, and in some cases killed by dominant ones. Close observation will allow you to isolate animals when necessary. Most of the small tortoises currently imported in the trade are not overly aggressive except during the spring breeding season.

Growth rings in a spurred tortoise. New shell is generated at the outer edges of the scutes. Photo by Chris Estep.

Acclimation

You should quarantine any newly obtained tortoise in an area
where no other tortoises or reptiles are kept. To introduce a newly
imported tortoise into an existing collection is to court disaster.
You should quarantine newly obtained tortoises for at least 90
days.

During the quarantine or acclimation period, keep your tortoise
in a simple enclosure with newspaper or newsprint as a substrate,
to allow for monitoring the status of the feces. Nearly all imported tortoises are infected with nematode worms. Many species, particularly those from tropical, humid countries, are also
infected with protozoan parasites such as *Entamoeba, Hexamita*
and *Trichomonas*. Without treatment infected tortoises usually die.

One reliable indicator of protozoan parasites is runny, watery
stools. This is often associated with dehydration, loss of weight,
loss of appetite and lethargy. Nematodes are commonly visible in
the stools of infected tortoises. Ideally, you will have a good
reptile veterinarian perform a fecal check for parasites and pre-
scribe the appropriate treatment. If you are unwilling to invest in
this expense, you can treat imported tortoises with Panacur®
(fenbendazole) at a dosage of 50 milligrams per kilogram (of body
weight). Repeat the treatment in two weeks.

For protozoan parasites, treat tortoises with Flagyl® (metronidazole) at a dosage of 50 milligrams per kilogram, and repeat in
four days. (This dosage applies to the actual weight of the tortoise; it is not a formula wherein the weight is divided in half to
account for shell weight.) Routine treatment using the above

13

medications will significantly increase the chances of survival in captivity of many tropical tortoises. If you decide to practice these treatments on your own, without the assistance of a veterinarian, you do so at your own risk. Errors of dosage, can cause reptile deaths. See *Understanding Reptile Parasites* by Roger Klingenberg (1993) for methods of administration. If a tortoise is eating, mixing the medications in its food is the easiest and least stressful method of administration.

During acclimation, monitor your tortoise for respiratory infections. You can easily diagnose discharge of mucus from the nostrils by gently pressing the ball of your thumb up against the throat area, which will usually cause mucus to emerge from the nostrils of tortoises with respiratory infections. Other symptoms of respiratory infection include watery eyes, gaping, and puffing of the throat area (signs of pneumonia). During the early stages of a respiratory infection, keeping the animal at the high range of its temperature requirements can allow a tortoise to fight off the infection on its own, but in chronic cases or when throat puffing or gaping is present, consult a veterinarian for treatment of the tortoise with antibiotics. Make sure you consult an experienced and reputable reptile veterinarian as inexperienced veterinarians can cause more harm than good.

You should closely monitor feeding, weight and behaviors in general during acclimation. If your tortoise proves to be healthy after the quarantine period is over, you can move it to more permanent quarters.

Housing

Whenever possible, you should house tortoises outdoors in suitable enclosures. You can easily construct vivaria of plywood or boards nailed to two-inch-by-four-inch posts. For small species, the walls of an enclosure should have a height at least twice the length of the largest tortoise. With large species, a height equal to the length of the shell is usually adequate. Some small tortoises are adept climbers; you must take care to assure that no vivarium structure or irregularities along the walls can provide them with opportunities to escape.

Several tortoise species are burrowers. Desert tortoises, Russian tortoises, and African spurred tortoises are burrowers during at least parts of the year. With these species, construct the walls of the enclosure or some type of barrier to extend at least one foot underground around the perimeter of the enclosure. You can make

Outdoor pens for pancake tortoises. Note the board on the right side to provide shelter from the sun and the clay tiles for ground shelters. The top was covered with plastic netting to keep out potential predators. Gray fox and raccoons can wipe out a colony of these tortoises overnight.

the walls out of marine plywood or wood, using a wood sealer to protect it against the elements. With smaller species of tortoises, frames of wood with fiberglass sheeting also work well. Brick or concrete block walls are good choices for all tortoises, particularly large species.

You should provide screen tops or shade cloth tops for all small species. These tops will keep out children and the many potential predators of tortoises. Depending on where you live, skunks, opossums, raccoons, coyotes, gray foxes, and dogs are all potential tortoise predators. Heed this warning. Waking up one morning to find all your prize tortoises or baby tortoises mauled and mangled is not a fun experience, and it will trigger a hindsight guilt trip ("I should have listened to Philippe's warning, but I was pretty sure there weren't any foxes around!").

Adults of large species of tortoises generally do a pretty good job of protecting themselves from attack by the more common predators. This means that you can usually keep adult specimens (not small juveniles) of African spurred, leopard, Burmese brown, and Galapagos tortoises in open-top enclosures.

Other enclosure alternatives include the large, round, watering-

A simple store setup for Russian tortoises. As a rule, tortoises are best kept and displayed in large wood frame enclosures, fiberglass enclosures, large plastic wading pools or plastic watering troughs rather than small glass tanks. Photo by Chris Estep.

16

An outdoor pen with a large heated shelter for housing a male and two female African spurred tortoises. Photo by Chris Wood.

trough-type (six feet in diameter or larger), partially buried in the ground and partially filled with soil or pits constructed with retaining walls.

Indoor enclosures
You can use very large, all glass aquaria or vivaria for keeping small species. Even better are custom-built wood enclosures in a corner of a room, or a children's large plastic wading pool. Whatever the choice, tortoises require a fair amount of space.

Loose in the yard
Keeping tortoises loose in the yard commonly invites neglect. The tortoises get lost, escape, are eaten or injured by predators, starve, or freeze to death. If a yard is fenced and regular monitoring is possible and carried out, then species adapted to the climate of your area may fare well. Regular feeding, however, is necessary, and there is always the risk that your pets will escape or be killed by predators such as dogs.

Size of enclosures
For keeping and breeding tortoises on a long-term basis, the very minimum size enclosure for one to three tortoises should be a *square footage* of the length of a tortoise multiplied by six. Thus, a six-inch-long tortoise requires a three-foot (six times six inches) by three-foot enclosure (nine-square-feet) enclosure. Personally, I think that a square footage formula that takes the length of a tortoise and multiplies it by eight is closer to an ideal minimum. Bigger is generally better, but an enclosure should not be so big that you cannot monitor the status of a tortoise. Because many

17

people do not want to build a square enclosure, a guideline is to use the same square footage, but with no side less than three times the length of a tortoise. These size requirements may be bad news to many new tortoise owners, but we must not keep animals without considering their quality of life. If you cannot provide a large enough enclosure, consider purchasing reptile species that fare better in smaller enclosures, such as leopard geckos or corn snakes.

Substrates

You can keep tortoises outdoors on a planted soil substrate where the surface remains dry. Few species of tortoise can tolerate permanently wet or soggy soil surfaces. Indoors, you can use newspaper; it has the advantage of allowing you to easily monitor the status of the stools and to replace the substrate when it is fouled. For tortoises that require higher relative humidity, you can lightly mist newspaper without it deteriorating. For many species you can use alfalfa pellets or rabbit pellets. They are absorbent and can be eaten by hungry tortoises.

Although I have read literature claiming that alfalfa pellets are potentially harmful because they swell if the tortoise drinks water, I have never seen a case in which ingestion of these pellets has presented a problem; in fact, alfalfa pellets make a good

Spurred tortoises are stubborn and intelligent creatures that quickly learn the access to heated shelters. Photo by Chris Estep.

18

component for the captive diet of many tortoises. I have raised several species of tortoises from hatchlings on alfalfa pellets without problems. On the other hand, if alfalfa pellets are allowed to get wet, mold may grow and could become a health hazard. You

A large pen with a heated shelter for keeping and breeding African spurred tortoises. Photo by Chris Estep.

should raise tortoises that require high humidity on an alternative medium because alfalfa pellets cannot be soaked. For some species, orchid (fir) bark or cypress mulch will work, particularly with species that require higher relative humidity, as you can mist down both of these substrates. Potting soil will work with forest species, although you should allow the surface to dry out. Sand or small pebbles can cause problems if they are ingested and are not recommended. Rough pebbles or rocks are a bad idea because they can abrade the tortoise's plastron.

Relative humidity
Outdoors relative humidity can be increased in dry climates by misting systems on timers. Indoors, cool air humidifiers will prove beneficial for species from tropical and humid climates.

Ventilation
Good air flow is recommended with all tortoises.

Monitoring equipment
All lighting should be set on timers so that the tortoises receive 12-14 hours of light during the warmer months of the year. During the winter only 10 hours of daylight will be necessary.

Thermometers should be used to monitor the temperature of the enclosures. For smaller indoor setups, the best are the electronic digital type thermometers with an external probe. These can be purchased mail-order or through electronic supply stores such as

19

Outdoor pens for large tortoises should be raked on a weekly basis to remove fecal material and left over food. Photo by Chris Estep.

Radio Shack®. The thermometer should be attached to the cool end of the enclosure and the probe at the warm end. Outdoors minimum/maximum display thermometers can be attached inside heated shelters as well as outside in a place sheltered from rain.

Heating systems should be connected to a thermostatic control. When possible (this depends on the amount of wattage)the pulse proportional thermostats such as Biostat® and Helix Controls® are a better choice than on-off type thermostats.

Smoke alarms

Smoke alarms should be installed in any room where reptiles are kept. They are recommended inside heated shelters for large tortoises.

A wood frame pen with fiberglass paneled walls and shade cloth used for housing small tortoises in southern California. Photo by Chris Wood.

Design and Landscaping

Shelters

All tortoises require some kind of shelter. You can easily construct these out of plywood and two by four inch studs. Basically, all you need is a box with an opening at one end that allows easy access. Large cork sections work well with small tortoises.

Flat rocks

Many tortoises develop excessively long nails on a soft substrate because of lack of wear. Placing some flattened rocks in the enclosure will facilitate normal nail wear.

Heating and Lighting

Heating

Tortoises kept outdoors can be kept warm by providing heated pens or houses. These can be heated with overhead incandescent

This insulated shelter is easily heated by a single hanging spotlight in a reflector type fixture. Photo by Chris Estep.

Outdoor planted open pens for tortoises. Photo by Chris Wood.

spotlights or infrared heating units such as the infrared bulbs and modules from RAM Network (preferable because they don't generate light and they are less likely to cause fires). The heating systems should be wired to an adjustable thermostat preferably with an alarm to warn of overheating or heater failure. In addition, a smoke alarm should be placed inside these heated shelters. Other heating alternatives for large tortoises are electric pig blankets which should also be connected to a thermostatic control system. Use pig blankets according to instructions to prevent burns and fires.

Indoors, spotlights, subtank reptile heaters, infrared ceramic heaters, and pig blankets can all be used to keep tortoises warm. All should be installed and used according to the manufacturer's instructions to prevent the risks of fire or thermal burns. As with other reptiles the idea is to provide a heat gradient that allows the animals to thermoregulate so heat should be provided only at one end of the enclosure. Heating systems should be connected to thermostats and a smoke alarm installed in the room where the tortoises are kept.

Lighting
Overhead lighting should be installed for tortoises kept indoors in addition to spotlights if they are the primary heat source. The new reptile high UVB fluorescent full spectrum bulbs such as ESU Reptile Daylight®, Hagen Repti-Glo® and Zoomed's Reptisun® UVB 5.0 are good choices for providing daytime lighting. Place lights on top of indoor enclosures so that the top of the shells are within less than twelve inches of the bulbs.

Plants

Small tortoises that are kept out-doors or indoors in large enclosures should have shrubs, bushes, and grass clumps to hide in or under. With large species you can use small trees or large shrubs. Out-doors, you can use jade plants, elephant bush, palms, large coarse grasses, mulberry, and many other plant species, depending upon where you live.

The interior of the pen showing plants. Photo by Chris Wood.

Vivarium enrichment

Tortoises in the wild do not live or lie in bare boxes. Make an effort to vary the topography of your vivarium; make the substrate sloped in some areas. Add flat rock, plants, cork bark sections, and sections of thick, flattened dried wood branches to make the environment more interesting. Your best inspiration for vivarium enrichment should be research on your tortoise's habitat. Experiment to simulate some of the essential elements of that habitat, but avoid landscape structures that can lead to your tortoise easily tipping over on its back; that means no steep climbing areas, no tall rocks, and no thick wood section that could cause a tortoise to fall backwards when attempting to climb it. Creating tunnels out of large pipe is one way of creating shelters for tortoises while at the same time enriching their environment.

A wood frame sunning enclosure with wire mesh to protect animals from predators and with shade cloth to reduce sun exposure. In addition, shelters are provided inside the pen. Photo by Chris Wood.

TORTOISES AND SWIMMING POOLS

Every year there are tales of tortoises drowning in swimming pools. If you have a pool, keep tortoises in secure pens and *not* loose in the yard.

Tortoises need shelter from excessive heat, sunlight and rain. These Russian tortoises are seeking shelter from the sun beneath a narrow board. Ideally more shelters should have been provided. Photo by Chris Wood.

Feeding and Watering

All tortoises are primarily vegetarians; a few are occasional carnivores or scavengers. The greatest concern with keeping tortoises is that, like humans on a vegetarian diet, they must be fed high quality foods to obtain all the nutrients, vitamins and minerals that their bodies require. Because tortoises are anatomically and physiologically built as vegetarians (with chambered stomachs and long intestines), excess protein can be harmful to their health. Most dietary problems of captive tortoises are caused by poor quality or low variety of vegetarian diet or by too much meat and protein in their diet.

A tortoise diet should consist of the following:
Mixed greens and grasses with high calcium content (about 80% of the total diet). Give two or more types per feeding. For hatchlings, chop the food into bite-size pieces (approximately the length of the head). For adults, tough fibrous foods, such as broccoli, should be chopped into bite-size pieces. Recommended mixed greens and grasses:

> Fresh clover, timothy alfalfa hay (for large species)
> Kale
> Collard and Mustard greens
> Clover
> Dandelion
> Romaine lettuce
> Beet and carrot tops
> Mulberry leaves
> Grass clippings
> Select weeds
> Select flowers, such as hibiscus and nasturtium

Miscellaneous fruits and vegetables (about 20% of the diet).
Offer three or more kinds daily.

> Grated or chopped carrots (depending on size of tortoise)
> Grated or chopped squashes (zucchini and yellow squash)
> Green beans
> Broccoli, chopped if necessary
> Raw corn, cut off the cob
> Tomatoes
> Figs
> Apricots
> Citrus fruit (oranges, lemons, tangerines)
> Papaya
> Pineapple
> Strawberries (small amounts only)
> Melons, particularly cantaloupe
> Other fruits and vegetables in season

High protein foods

Red-footed, Burmese brown, elongated and hinge-back tortoises
should be offered high protein foods such as low fat dog food,
monkey chow, cooked egg and baby mice to make up about 10%
of the diet. Other tortoises and baby tortoises can be offered up to
5% high protein foods.

Three African spurred tortoises (Geochelone sulcata) hatched from the same clutch at five months of age. The smallest specimen was part of a group of five animals fed only greens and vegetables, the middle specimens in a group fed a mix of greens and vegetables with equal amounts of ZuPreem low fat monkey chow and the largest specimen on the right was in the group fed exclusively ZuPreem monkey chow. The size differences are representative of the effects of their diets. The four inch shell length required for legal commercial sale in the United States was achieved by five months from hatching. Photo by Chris Wood.

Note: Do not give excessive amounts of legumes such as peas or lima beans.

Vitamin and mineral supplementation

Tortoises kept outdoors and fed a varied diet need their diet supplemented with calcium carbonate powder, sprinkled or mixed into their food two to three times a week. By weight their diet should be supplemented at a ratio of 1% with calcium carbonate. Once a month supplement with a vitamin/mineral mix.

For tortoises kept indoors, supplement their diet three times a week with calcium carbonate (1% of diet by weight) and lightly every one to two weeks with a powdered reptile multivitamin and mineral supplement containing vitamin D3 such as Reptivite®, Herptivite® or Vionate®. The liberal coating of diets with high D3 supplements such as RepCal® can be harmful and is not recommended by this author for tortoises.

Commercial diets

Available now are commercial pelleted diets that are useful for raising baby tortoises. These products claim to provide the nutrients needed for healthy growth, including vitamins and minerals. However, the current view is that these diets have not yet been tested with regards to long term effects and some caution is warranted until this has been accomplished. Some of these new commercial tortoise diets are being formulated for the raising of tortoises at all stages of life. Initially you may have to soak or mix the pellets with greens and vegetables to get the tortoises started on the diet. Providing 50% mixed greens and vegetables in addition to a commercial diet is a good idea. Make water available to your tortoise at all times when feeding it on commercial diets.

Note: High quality human vitamin/mineral supplements such as Centrum® can be crushed with mortar and pestle and provide more trace elements than reptile vitamins on the market. Dosage = 2 tablets per 150 lbs of tortoise weekly.

The leopard tortoise is an herbivore best raised on grasses and high calcium lettuces and a variety of chopped vegetables. Imported specimens that are initially reluctant to feed can often be coaxed by offering squashes. Photo by Chris Estep.

Vionate® is a low concentration supplement which can be used more liberally i.e. sprinkling over food than other vitamin/ mineral supplements.

Feeding your baby tortoises soaked monkey biscuits such as the ZuPreem® low-fat, high-fiber primate diet will result in good growth for the first year (with no pyramiding of the carapace); however, cut down on the monkey chow to no more than ten percent of the diet after one year and five percent after two years. Until research leads to commercial diet formulations that can assure longevity and long-term health, it is best to offer a varied diet to adults, including these commercial diets as merely one component. Why experiment with your animals?

Feeding the big ones
Large specimens of tortoises such as African spurred, leopard, or Galapagos tortoises can be expensive to feed. One alternative is to offer them fresh clover hay, timothy hay or freshly soaked alfalfa hay to make up as much as three quarters of their diet. If you live in an area where spineless prickly pear can be grown, this is a cheap supplemental food source that large tortoises like. You also should feed large tortoises a variety of vegetables and fruits. Offer

carrots and cantaloupe, which are good sources of vitamin A, on a regular basis.

How often should you feed tortoises?
Except during the months when certain species of tortoises are hibernating, you should offer tortoises food every one to two days.

Feeding baby tortoises
You should chop food in small pieces that are easy for baby tortoises to eat. The commercial diets are a good way to prevent some of the problems associated with insufficient calcium and vitamin D3 during the first two years of raising tortoises.

> Cuttle bones placed soft side up in an enclosure with baby tortoises are an excellent source of calcium. Tortoises will nip out pieces as they need it.

Pyramiding and disproportionate growth of the shell
Tortoises, when not provided with enough heat and fed excessive calcium, vitamin D3, and/or protein, may develop deformed shells. This deformity commonly takes the form of pyramiding of the scutes, but an overgrown shell, too thick and too large for the body size of the animal, may also develop. This disproportionate growth may be linked to protein availability in relation to calcium and D3, but temperature is now considered a critical factor with this syndrome. At the higher metabolic rates associated with a

Ontogenic changes in shell pattern of the pancake tortoise. Photo by Micki and Brad Dutenhoeffer.

high temperature source such as a spotlight or heated floor, pyramiding will usually not occur. Offering a balanced diet *and* providing a heat source thus appears critical for successfully raising healthy tortoises. A different set of problems (metabolic bone disease) may occur if you do not provide enough heat, calcium, vitamin D3, or sunlight.

Water

Have clean water available at all times in a shallow container that allows a tortoise to dip its head down and drink. Deep containers not easily reached by tortoises are useless. For babies, jar lids or the lids of plastic storage boxes work well. As the animals get older, you can use large containers, including shallow food-storage containers, and later, large pans and/or plastic containers.

It is important that the water be kept clean and that the container be disinfected regularly with a five-percent bleach solution (soaked for 30 minutes to an hour, then thoroughly rinsed). Foul water can be a vector for the spread of disease.

A hatchling African spurred tortoise (Geochelone sulcata). This species is now bred by the thousands annually in the United States. Photo by Chris Wood.

Hibernation (Brumation)

General guidelines for hibernation

1. Hibernate only healthy animals. Give appropriate treatment to lightweight specimens and sick specimens, and postpone their hibernation for a year if necessary.

2. For two weeks prior to hibernation, stop feeding your tortoises, allowing time for the emptying of their gastrointestinal (GI) tract. Tortoises hibernated with food in their intestines can develop serious GI problems. Hydrate tortoises prior to hibernation.

3. Hibernate hatchlings and immature animals only for a short term, usually between one and two months. Adults can hibernate up to four months. Many herpetoculturists forego hibernation the first one or two years of a small tortoise's life. Hibernation is

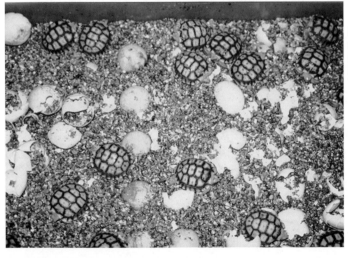

Hatching African spurred tortoises (Geochelone sulcata). Photo by Chris Wood.

"I got my eye on you." Few things are more endearing than hatching tortoises. Photo by Chris Wood.

definitely required by the third or fourth year if you want a long-lived, healthy, and breeding temperate climate tortoise.

You should allow tortoises from temperate climates (such as European tortoises or Russian tortoises) to hibernate if they are to breed and fare well for a long time. In areas of the country that are very cold in the winter, this usually means setting the tortoises up in a hibernation pen in a garage where the temperature drops into the 60s and 50s° F (10 to 20.6° C), but does not get near freezing. In addition to a deep layer of a flaky substrate (such as soil, orchid bark, and shredded moss), provide a mulch of leaves or hay for the tortoises to burrow into or under. Always have a dish of clean water available during the course of hibernation. In areas of the United States with mild winters, such as southern California, you can keep most of the European tortoises outdoors year-round. Simply provide a pile of hay for them to burrow into if needed. You should expose tropical and subtropical tortoises to a shorter photoperiod during the winter (ten hours of light per day) and to temperatures 5 to 10° F (2.8 to 5.6° C) cooler than average. If kept outdoors, these species need heated shelters, and you must monitor them to make sure that they are in their shelters during cold spells.

Make sure that you provide light above the substrate, and monitor your animals to be sure that they are healthy and do not develop respiratory infections. Water should be available in shallow pans at all times during hibernation. After activity resumes, make sure water dishes are available for tortoises to drink. Generally, three months of hibernation is adequate for most adult temperate species.

Notes on Various Species

African spurred tortoise *(Geochelone sulcata)*

The African spurred tortoise gets large and grows quickly (up to twelve inches in length within two years). Unless you are prepared to offer the room-size enclosures that these tortoises eventually require, they may not be your best choice. They are, however, among the hardiest of the tortoises.

Size: African spurred tortoises grow to a length of about two feet, occasionally larger in the case of males. Adults weigh between 100 and 120 pounds, although there are records of males of certain populations exceeding 200 pounds.

Sexing: Adult males develop a recurved anterior margin of the carapace. They have a concave plastron, elongated and enlarged gular scutes, and a longer tail. The anal scute angle of males are wider than that of females, so it can be used as an indicator in sexing young animals.

African spurred tortoise feeding on kale. Photo by Chris Wood.

Housing: These large tortoises eventually require large pens; the equivalent of at least 16 feet by 16 feet for a trio, and larger is preferable. Wood frames should extend 1-2 feet underground.

Temperature: African spurred tortoises should have access to a basking light while they are young, with a basking site temperature of 95° F (35° C). Background temperature should be in the 80's° F (26.7 to 31.7° C) during the day. At night it can drop to as low as 70° F (21.1° C). Adults safely tolerate night drops into the 60's° F (15.6 to 20.6° C). During the winter, daytime temperatures can be 5 to 10° F (2.8 to 5.6° C) cooler, but a basking site of 85 to 90° F (29.4 to 48.3° C) is recommended. Most breeders provide heated shelters during the winter.

Diet: The African spurred is an herbivorous tortoise; thus, high-fiber grasses should form the bulk of its diet. Soaked alfalfa hay or clover hay can make up a significant proportion of the diet of adults. Also offer them squashes, cabbages, dark-green lettuces, broccoli, carrots, melons, and other plant matter. Babies can be fed standard baby tortoise diet.

Hibernation/prebreeding conditioning: For African "spurs," no hibernation is required, but many breeders allow a period of rest in the winter, with a decreased photoperiod and a 5 to 10° F (2.8 to 5.6° C) drop in temperature from daytime to nighttime. Some "spurs" lay eggs during the late winter or early spring, and thus you should closely monitor them during that period. They breed easily, with copulation usually occurring during hot days and months of the year (at least in southern California) and egg-laying

Herman's tortoise (Testudo hermanni). This tortoise is now available almost exclusively as captive-bred specimens. This is a nice tortoise. It grows relatively large but not so large that housing presents any special difficulties. It is attractive, hardy, easy to breed and demonstrates a significant degree of responsiveness toward human keepers. It can be kept like the spur-thigh tortoise.

34

usually occurring during the following late winter or spring. Clutch size can number more than 30 eggs, but it is typically between 20 and 30 eggs. Young females may lay smaller clutch sizes. One to three clutches of eggs are laid per breeding season.

Incubation: At a temperature of 84 to 86° F (28.9 to 30° C), incubation can be as short as 92 days, but more typically it is 120 to 160 days. Some eggs may take even longer to hatch. The general philosophy on incubating African spurred tortoise eggs is to leave them in the incubator until you are certain that they have gone bad.

CARRION FLIES
In many areas of the United States carrion flies are a pest that will lay eggs and colonize on tortoise eggs as soon as they are cracked at hatching time. The maggots can invade the yolk and kill hatchling tortoises. Monitor incubating containers carefully for carrion flies. Transfer eggs to new containers when needed. Carrion fly maggots in the yolk sac of hatchling tortoises can be flushed out with hydrogen peroxide or Betadine® solution.

Spur-thigh tortoise *(Geochelone ibera)*
The spur-thigh tortoise, a temperate species, is occasionally imported in large numbers from Turkey. They are often sold on the United States. market as Greek tortoises. After an initial treatment for parasites, these tortoises tend to be hardy and

The spur-thigh tortoise (Testudo ibera) is occasionally imported in some numbers into the United States. Care is similar to Herman's tortoises. Imports are often heavily parasitized and must be treated if they are to establish in captivity.

adaptable, and in time they can become quite tame. They have a lot of personality. If you provide them with a dry substrate and moderate relative humidity, this is an easy species to keep.

Sexing: Males are smaller than females. Their tails are longer than females with a horny terminal tip.

Size: Up to about 7 1/2 inches (19 cm), although usually less than 6 inches (15.2 cm)

Diet: Standard vegetarian tortoise fare.

Breeding: This species breeds readily if allowed to hibernate in the 50's° F. Clutch size can range from four to twelve. Up to two clutches a year.

Russian tortoise (*Testudo horsfieldii*)

The Russian tortoise, a burrowing species, is currently imported in some numbers from Russia. We hope that management policies can prevent over collection and lack of control of them as a renewable resource, a pattern that has had an impact on other species collected in large numbers for the pet trade. (Unfortunately, there is too much greed, misguided legislation, and short-term thinking to make this likely.) These are hardy, spunky, and responsive animals, and they rank among this author's favorite species. Keep them in dry vivaria; they are tolerant of a wide range of temperatures, but they breed successfully only if they are hibernated at relatively cool temperatures (50's° F) for two to three months.

Imported Russian tortoises (Testudo horsfieldii) feeding on mulberry leaves. The shells of imports are often worn or with signs of surface damage. This tortoise digs burrows so walls must be buried deep into the ground or a screen barrier placed 24 inches below ground to prevent escapes. This is a hardy and responsive tortoise that requires hibernation at cool (50° F) temperatures for successful captive-breeding.

Sexing: Males are smaller and with longer tails than females.

Size: Up to 8 inches (20.3 cm).

Care: Russian tortoises are hardy if they are kept in dry vivaria. This species digs burrows; thus, the walls of outdoor vivaria must extend into the ground at least twelve inches. Shrubs and grass clumps are recommended. Use loose alfalfa hay to provide shelter and an area for your tortoise to dig into during excessively hot or cool weather.

Diet: Standard tortoise fare including fresh cut grasses.

Temperature: Very tolerant of a range of temperatures from low 90's° F in summer to 40's° F in winter as long as they can burrow.

Breeding: In the United States, the breeding of this species has been sporadic. Hibernation at cool temperatures appears to be essential. Egg-laying is a rather quick process, so owners often miss eggs laid in an outdoor pen. Clutch size ranges from two to six and up to three clutches may be laid during a breeding season. Babies are large, spunky, aggressive, delightful creatures. Incubation time at a temperature of 84 to 86° F (28.9 to 30° C) is about two months. At cooler temperatures, incubation can take as long as four months.

Marginated tortoise (*Testudo marginata*)
The marginated tortoise is the largest of the European tortoises. It is a hardy and impressive species and is regularly available as captive-bred babies.

Size: Females up to about 10 inches (25.4 cm); males up to 12 inches (30.4 cm).

Sexing: Males have a narrower "waist" than females, more flared margins and longer tails.

Care: The marginated tortoises are hardy and can be kept like Herman's tortoises.

Hibernation: Hibernation in the 50's° F and low 60's° F for two to three months is recommended for this species. It can be kept outdoors year round in mild climate areas of the United States such as southern California.

Breeding: The marginated tortoise breeds readily in captivity, laying several clutches of eight to ten eggs per year. Incubate them like African spurred tortoises. At a temperature of 85° F

A young marginated tortoise (Testudo marginata). This species is currently bred in small numbers by United States hobbyists. When young they are light colored but get darker as they mature. This is the largest of the European tortoises growing up to almost a foot in length.

(29.4° C), eggs hatch in 60 to 80 days. Sexual maturity is reached in seven to nine years.

Leopard tortoise (Geochelone pardalis)

The leopard tortoise is one of the most beautiful of the large tortoises. It is still imported in some numbers from Africa. Mortality rates in imports can be high if they are not hydrated and treated for parasites. Remove ticks from imports by applying rubbing alcohol to the tick and then removing it with tweezers or forceps. Captive-bred babies, mostly of *Geochelone pardalis babcocki* are regularly available.

Size: This is the second-largest tortoise of Africa after the African spurred tortoise, growing to a maximum size of 21 inches (53.3 cm). More typically, specimens are around 15 inches.

Sexing: Females are typically smaller than males. Males have a concave plastron and a longer and thicker tail than females.

Diet: Like the African spurred tortoise, this herbivorous tortoise species should be offered high-fiber grasses and greens as a primary component of its diet. A common cause of death in captivity is excess protein in the diet, which leads to gout. Also, avoid oversupplementation with vitamin D3.

Care: Similar to that of the African spurred tortoise.

Breeding: This species is relatively easy to breed, but the best reported success has been with specimens kept outdoors in Arizona and California. Female leopard tortoises can lay multiple clutches from eight to more than 20 eggs per clutch. Incubate them like you would the African spurred tortoise. Incubation can vary from four and a half months to more than a year, depending on a variety of factors such as the origins of the breeding stock. Captive-raised specimens may breed by as early as four and a

Leopard tortoises (Geochelone pardalis babcocki). This is a large, beautiful and readily available species which can be produced on a commercial scale. The sculptured appearing shell with pyramidal scutes of these specimens although attractive to some is a phenomenon of captivity usually associated with unbalanced diets. It is also probable that in the wild, greater wear and tear of shell surfaces contribute to the more rounded appearance of wild collected animals. Photo by Chris Estep.

half years if they are raised under optimal conditions. More typically, captive-raised females first breed when they are between five and seven years of age. Imported adult animals may take from one to three years to "cycle in" and breed regularly. Captive-raised animals tend to be more consistent breeders than wild-caught specimens.

Hingeback tortoises (Kinixys)
These African tortoises have a hinged carapace that can offer additional protection to the tail and hind legs when they are attacked by a potential predator.

Bells's hingeback (Kinixys belliana)
Bell's hingeback tortoises are occasionally imported from East Africa and is tolerant of drier conditions than *K. erosa*. Most can be kept the same way as leopard tortoises, but they require well-planted vivaria with shelters. Relative humidity should be 70%-90%. Hingebacks prefer green vegetables and fruit, and should also be offered low fat dog food, earthworms or a soaked chow (10% of total diet). These tortoises are secretive and not the best choice if you are interested in a responsive, personable animal. Generally, they are more difficult to keep long term than many of the other commonly imported species. They are best left to specialists.

Bell's hingeback tortoise (Kinixys belliana). Photo by Micki and Brad Dutenhoeffer.

Forest hingeback *(Kinixys erosa)*

This beautiful tortoise is not recommended for inexperienced tortoise keepers. Forest hingebacks require large enclosures with moderate to high relative humidity. Imports are typically heavily parasitized, dehydrated, and stressed, and their mortality rate tends to be high. They are generally considered to be a delicate species.

Size: Males up to 12 inches (30.4 cm), females up to 10 inches (25.4 cm). Do not keep adult males together, as they may fight and bite each other. A male can be kept with several females.

Acclimation: Deparasitization, hydration, and the minimizing of stress are critical.

Housing: These moderately large tortoises require large vivaria with a substrate of soil, soil and orchid bark mix, or cypress mulch. High humidity, a shelter, and plants are required for this shy species. Because these tortoises come from tropical forests, they do not tolerate cold and should be maintained at temperatures ranging in the upper 70's° F to low 80's° F (25 to 28° C).

Diet: Feed them leafy greens, chopped soft fruit, vegetables, and mushrooms. They also eat some meat, including canned dog food

Pancake tortoises (Malacochersus tornieri) breeding. Because of its small size, the pancake tortoise is one of the best species for accommodating indoors. Unfortunately, they have a low reproductive rate and few are produced annually by breeders.

and soaked monkey chow, as well as invertebrates such as snails, earthworms, and pinched king mealworms *(Zophobas).*

Pancake tortoise *(Malacochersus tornieri)*
Pancake tortoises have been imported occasionally in relatively large numbers from East Africa, but they are now protected in most of their range and are seldom available anymore. They are found in rocky habitats. This relatively small species is a good choice for people with limited space or indoor facilities. It is critical that breeding populations be established by herpeto-culturists if this species is to continue to be available. The pancake tortoise has many qualities including small size and interesting behaviors that could make it an ideal tortoise pet. Unfortunately, the reproductive rate of this species is rather low, with females laying one to two eggs at about two-month intervals.

Size: Up to 6 inches (15.2 cm).

Sexing: Males have longer tails and slightly broader heads than females. Females are typically more patterned than males.

Housing: A vivarium of at least two feet by four feet is recommended for this species. A dry substrate is required. Use stacked shelters of large flattened rocks and/or cork bark sections to create a varied landscape.

Diet: A mixed diet of greens, freshly cut grasses, and vegetables is recommended. Generally, pancake tortoises do not eat fruit, but cantaloupe is the exception.

Temperature: This is a high-altitude species with significant day-to-night temperature fluctuations. Turning off all heat sources at night is a good idea, as long as night temperatures are in the 60's° F (15.6 to 20.6° C). Night-temperature drops into the low 60's° F (15.6 to 17.2° C) are recommended for successful breeding. Daytime temperatures should be in the low to mid 80's° F (26.7 to 29.5° C). Reducing the photoperiod during the winter is also recommended.

Breeding: There has been increased success with captive breeding of this species. Success depends on having groups of tortoises from the same area of collections. It is best to purchase all breeding stock from the same group of imports. In large enclosures, groups of this species can be maintained. Males will fight during the breeding season. Females lay one to two eggs per clutch up to six times a year. At 80-88° F eggs take 113 to 221 days to hatch.

Burmese brown tortoise (*Manouria emys*)

The Burmese brown is regarded as one of the most primitive of the living tortoises. It has characteristics of both a tortoise and a wood turtle. Generally, these are responsive and rather intelligent tortoises. Imported specimens are typically dehydrated and highly parasitized, and their mortality rate tends to be high; however, there are now several breeders in Florida who have captive-bred animals available on a regular basis. If you want a large, responsive pet tortoise, you should definitely consider captive-bred Burmese browns. The author's favorite tortoise besides Galapagos'.

Size: Up to nearly 2 feet (60 cm).

Sexing: Males tend to be larger than females and have proportionately larger heads. Males have longer tails.

The author's Burmese brown tortoises (Manouria emys phayrei), young female on left with adult male on right. These are the largest of the Asian tortoises and require large enclosures when adult. They are also one of the great tortoises in terms of personality and responsiveness. Although imports should be left to specialists because of the problems with establishing them to captivity, captive-bred animals are highly recommended for anyone wishing to eventually own a large tortoise pet.

Housing: Adults require at least an eight-foot by sixteen-foot enclosure. This species likes moderate to high relative humidity.

Temperature: In the low to mid 80's° F (26.8 to 28.3° C) during the day and the 70's° F (21.1 to 26.1° C) at night. During the winter, this species tolerates nighttime temperatures in the 60's° F (15.6 to 20.6° C), but they do not tolerate very high heat. Animals kept outdoors during heat waves should have access to shaded areas, insulated shelters, and cooling by misting systems. Bring them indoors during heat waves if you cannot provide these safeguards.

Diet: Burmese browns like a little more animal protein in their diet than do other tortoises, so offer occasional low fat dog food or soaked ZuPreem® monkey chow blocks; they prefer vegetables, greens and fruit to grasses.

Water: This species requires large shallow tubs or pools of water.

Breeding: The Burmese brown is bred by a few herpetoculturists, primarily in Florida. A large nest of leaves or other kind of litter is formed by the female. A single clutch of 23 and up to 51 eggs is laid annually.

Elongated tortoise (Indotestudo)
This pretty species with a cream yellow head contrasted with dark eyes is still imported occasionally from Southeast Asia. The elongated tortoise is generally hardy after it is deparasitized. In terms of personality, imported animals often display a certain indifference. Well-planted vivaria with high humidity (75%-90%) and moderate warmth are recommended for them. Substrates of peat moss and orchid bark are suitable. Captive-bred hatchlings, which are sometimes available from Florida breeders, tend to be more personable.

Size: Up to 13 inches (33 cm).

Sexing: Males have longer and thicker tails than the females; they also have a deeper anal notch than the females.

Housing: This tortoise requires moderately high relative humidity and moderate heat, in the upper 70's° F to low 80's° F (25 to 28.3° C) during the day. At night the temperature can drop safely to the low 70's° F (21.1 to 22.8° C). During the winter they can tolerate a 5° F (2.8° C) drop in range, but you should make available a warm spot for thermoregulation.

Diet: Elongated tortoises fare well on a standard vegetarian diet of mixed vegetables and fruit, as well as occasional meat, slugs, and earthworms.

Breeding: This species lays up to three clutches of two to nine eggs. Incessant ramming by males is a common complaint when groups of these tortoises are kept together. A male with one to three females in large enclosures is a good sex ratio.

Star tortoise (*Geochelone elegans*)
The star tortoise species is occasionally imported in small numbers. More rarely, captive-bred babies are available. It is one of the comparatively expensive species on the market, and its low reproductive rate and increasing rarity are unlikely to change its high price. One of the most beautifully patterned tortoises in the world, the star tortoise's cost and the potential high mortality rate of imported specimens make this a tortoise for the experienced keeper.

Acclimation: If star tortoises are parasitized, particularly hatchlings or small specimens, their death rate tends to be quite high. In general, this is considered to be a rather difficult tortoise to

A two year old star tortoise (Geochelone elegans) captive-raised by the author. This species ranks among the most beautiful of the tortoises.

45

keep long term, but many tortoise specialists have had good luck with this species.

Size: Up to 13 inches, but most captive specimens are considerably smaller, usually around 8 inches (20.3 cm).

Housing: Star tortoises do best in a dry enclosure. They should be kept outdoors during the warmer months of the year in planted outdoor vivaria. Excessively damp or cool conditions have proven detrimental to this sensitive tortoise.

Temperature: Daytime in the low 80s° F (26.8 to 28.3° C) with a basking spot. Nighttime in the 70s° F (21.1 to 26.1° C). During the winter a 5-10° F (2.8 to 5.6° C) drop in temperature, as well as a reduced photoperiod, is recommended for two to three months. Always provide a heat source such as a basking light or (if the tortoise is kept outdoors) a heated shelter. Carefully monitor tortoises for respiratory infections at all times.

Diet: Star tortoises will feed on a standard tortoise diet cut to a size that they can ingest easily.

Breeding: Daily periods of rain or spraying can help elicit breeding behavior. To date, the star tortoise has been bred by only a few herpetoculturists. It can lay from one to four clutches of two to ten eggs. At 84-88° F eggs will hatch in 111-150 days.

Red-footed tortoise (Geochelone carbonaria)
The red-footed tortoise is decidedly one of the most beautiful, as well as one of the most personable, of the tortoises. Many tortoise keepers rank the red-footed tortoise among their favorite species. The red-foot is still occasionally imported in small numbers from South America, along with the yellow-footed tortoise. They are also bred in small numbers, mostly in Florida. After they are deparasitized, they become hardy. To fare well they require dry-surface substrates with moderate to high relative humidity. In dry areas you should increase the relative humidity by using misting systems outdoors or humidifiers indoors, in order to provide higher humidity.

This tropical tortoise does not tolerate excessively cool temperatures for long periods of time. Daytime temperatures should be in the low 80's° F (26.8 to 28.3° C) and nighttime temperatures in the mid 70's° F (23.3 to 24.4° C). In the winter, do not allow the temperature to drop more than 5° F (2.8° C) from this range. Respiratory infections and other diseases afflict these tortoises if they are kept too cool.

Size: Up to 12 inches (30.4 cm), but there are also larger forms that grow up to 16 inches (40.6 cm) and dwarf forms that seldom exceed 10 inches (25.4 cm).

Sexing: Males have a concave plastron, longer tail and narrow "waist".

Diet: The red-footed tortoise prefers greens and fruits and vegetables to grasses; they occasionally like meat or higher protein sources in their diet. They will appreciate a little dog food or soaked monkey biscuit once a week. A varied diet is important.

Temperature: Red-footed tortoises are best kept warm, in the 80's° F (26.8 to 31.6° C) during the day at moderate to moderately high relative humidity (70-85%).

Breeding: Red-foots are being bred with increasing frequency in the United States, particularly by Florida herpetoculturists. Spring and summer rain, or spraying, can help elicit breeding behavior. The red-footed tortoise lays several clutches of three to six relatively large eggs.

Red-footed tortoise (Geochelone carbonaria). This is one of the most attractive and responsive tortoises. Although they should be kept in dry enclosures they require a 70%-85% relative humidity. A higher percentage of fruit is required in their diet and they occasionally like meat protein although this should not be overdone.

47

Diseases and Disorders

Tortoises are among the more treatable of reptiles, and increasing numbers of reptile veterinarians are now qualified to treat them. Because of the nature of this book, which is meant to be condensed and introductory, we present only a brief outline of the more common tortoise diseases.

Dietary Problems
If you follow the instructions in this book, problems such as dietary deficiencies and metabolic bone disease should not occur in your tortoise collection.

Parasites
Ticks: Round, flattened, and usually shiny invertebrates, typically attached to soft skin parts. Apply rubbing alcohol to ticks, wait five minutes, and remove them with tweezers or forceps.

Internal parasites: Nematodes (roundworms) in feces accompanied by failure to gain weight. Treat with Panacur® (fenbendazole) at 50 milligrams per kilogram of body weight. Repeat in 10 days. All tortoises should be checked annually for parasites.

Protozoan parasites: Runny and/or bloody stools, weight loss, listlessness. Confirm diagnosis with a fecal exam by a qualified veterinarian. Treat the tortoise with Flagyl® (metronidazole) at 50 milligrams per kilogram of body weight. Repeat in 10 days. Keep the tortoises well hydrated. A veterinary consultation is recommended if you are an inexperienced tortoise keeper.

Respiratory infections

Symptoms include listlessness, closed or watery eyes, bubbly mucus emerging from nostrils, gaping, and gasping. If the symptoms are mild, attempt heat treatment keeping a tortoise in the higher range of it's temperature requirements. If the tortoise is listless, gaping, and demonstrating forced exhalation, consult a veterinarian immediately for treatment with injectable antibiotics. Some tortoise populations harbor resistant viruses that cause chronic respiratory infections. As a rule, tortoises from different locations should never be kept in close proximity to each other. You must quarantine all newly acquired tortoises; this point cannot be emphasized enough.

Septicemia

Listlessness, crushed-plastron damage with subshell bleeding, closed eyes, loss of muscular vigor are probable signs of septicemia, a fatal blood infection. Consult a qualified veterinarian for antibiotic treatment immediately.

Shell rot

If the plastron is injured and tortoises are kept on moist and/or soiled substrates bacterial infections of the shell may develop which can result in deep and potentially fatal pits in the bony shell or in septicemia. Such infections are visible as dark brown stains in the plastral area accompanied by lifting of epithelial scutes. To treat this, first keep the tortoise on a clean dry substrate such as newspaper. Then lift the edge of the epithelial scute to expose the infected area and apply Betadine solution to the infected areas every one to two days. In severe cases, veterinary attention should be sought immediately.

Swollen limbs and lumps

Swollen limbs, cheeks and the sudden development of lumps are all signs of probable infection. This will often require incising the infected area and removing caseous infected matter followed by flushing with Betadine and treatment with antibiotics. Except for the experienced, consulting a qualified veterinarian is recommended. Do not delay treatment.

See Recommended Reading section for references on the topic of diseases.

Salmonella and Hygiene

Although cases of salmonellosis linked to tortoises are very rare, tortoises can be carriers of salmonella. For this reason, common-sense hygienic practices are essential when keeping tortoises.

1. Always wash your hands after handling tortoises.

2. Tell children to wash their hands if they touch tortoises, never to put their hands in their mouths while handling tortoises, and never to kiss tortoises.

3. Do not let tortoises loose in your house; fecal smears in your home can increase the spread of disease.

4. Do not wash utensils, enclosures, or other items used with your tortoises at sinks or tubs used by your family members. If doing this is unavoidable, disinfect the area after use with a five-percent bleach solution.

5. Do not allow your tortoises to soak in sinks or tubs used by you or your family. This is common-sense hygiene.

SALMONELLA
Like some other reptiles, tortoises can be asymptomatic carriers of salmonella. Tortotises with runny or bloody feces should be checked by a veterinarian, but tortoises with no obvious signs of disease may also harbor salmonella bacteria.

Unwanted Tortoises

If you decide you can no longer keep your tortoise, you have several options. One is to advertise and offer your animal for sale in your local newspaper, in herpetological newsletters, or in herpetocultural periodicals such as *Reptiles*, *Reptiles USA*, or *Reptile and Amphibian Hobbyist*. If you are limited on time, another option is to sell or donate your tortoise back to the store from which you bought it or to another store that sells reptiles. (You will be offered a wholesale price, not retail, for your specimen.) Other options include adoption departments of herpetological societies, donations to schools, or giving your animal to an animal control center or a local humane society.

Under no circumstances should you *ever* release a captive animal in the wild. Not only will your animal have only a slight chance of survial, but there is always the risk that a disease or virus harbored by your tortoise could infect other tortoise or turtle populations. **Never release captive reptiles.**

Recommended Reading

Ernst, C.H. and R.W. Barbour. 1989. Turtles of the World. Smithsonian Institution Press. 313 pp. An essential reference on taxonomy, distribution and natural history of turtles including tortoises with many black and white and some color photos.

Highfield, A.C. 1990. Keeping and Breeding Tortoises in Captivity. R and A Publishing, Avon, England. 149 pp. This book is considered expensive by some but the value of information is well worth the price. Highly recommended.

Highfield, A.C. 1996. The Practical Encyclopedia of Keeping and Breeding Tortoises and Freshwater Turtles. Carapace Press, London, England. 295 pp. Distributed in the U.S. by Serpent's Tale, Excelsior, MN and Krieger Publishing, Melbourne, FL. An essential reference for the serious turtle keeper by one of the best author's on the subject.

Paull, R.C. The Eight Great Tortoises. Green Nature Books, Homestead, FL 33033. A self-published, photocopied and somewhat expensive book. Also opinionated, daring, personal and full of bits and pieces of practical information that only an experienced tortoise keeper could convey. I liked this book and recommend it to anyone keeping the larger tortoises.

Reptile Medicine Reading

Frye, F.L. 1991. Biomedical and Surgical Aspects of Captive Reptile Husbandry. 2.Vol. Krieger Publishing, Melbourne, FL. This is the primary reference work on the subject. Although expensive and aimed more at veterinarians than the herpetoculturist, serious tortoise keepers will find this a worthwhile investment. A must for any reptile veterinarian.

Mader, D. 1996. Reptile Medicine and Surgery. W.B. Saunders Company. 512 pp. This book covers a range of topics which I consider essential knowledge for any serious herpetoculturist. In terms of nutrition and reptile medicine, it is one of the most useful books on the market and one of the best published to date on the subject. Highly recommended notably the section on nutrition by Susan Donoghue and Julie Langenberg plus the sections on turtles and tortoises by Thomas Boyer and Donal Boyer.

Index

About the Author

Photo by Davina Colvin

Philippe de Vosjoli is the highly acclaimed author and publisher of the best-selling reptile-care books, The Herpetocultural Library Series®. His work in the field of herpetoculture has been recognized nationally and internationally for establishing high standards for amphibian and reptile care. His books, articles, guidelines and other writings have been praised and recommended by numerous herpetological societies, veterinarians and other experts in the field. Philippe de Vosjoli, was also the cofounder and president of The American Federation of Herpetoculurists, and was given the Josef Laszlo Memorial Award in 1995 for his excellence in herpetoculture and his contribution to the advancement of the field.

The Herpetocultural Library series®

The most comprehensive and precise information available for the care and breeding of your reptiles.

Learn all the "secrets" from the "masters". You'll find special tips and advice along with fundamental information detailed with the accuracy that you've come to expect ONLY from The Herpetocultural Library Series. Learn the techniques necessary for proper maintenance, breeding, feeding, housing, lighting, temperature requirements, supplementation, incubation and the rearing of juveniles. You'll also find sections on disease and treatments, various morphs and more!

Ask for the following titles at Book Stores and Pet Stores **EVERYWHERE!**

Can't find a title? Contact us directly at:

Advanced Vivarium Systems
P.O. Box 6050,
Mission Viejo, CA 92690

Call Toll-Free 1-800-982-9410   **www.avsbooks.com**

BD 0409	Bearded Dragons
LP 0307	Leopard Geckos
CB 0412	Care & Breeding of Chameleons
BP 0302	Ball Python Manual
IG 0404	Green Iguana Manual
TS 0402	Tarantulas & Scorpions
MT 0415	Monitors & Tegus
GA 0112	Green Anoles
RS 0110	Red-Eared Sliders
PT 0204	Popular Tortoises

CALL TOLL-FREE 1-877-4AVS-BOOK

GS 0203	Garter Snakes
TF 0304	Tree Frogs
BT 0303	Box Turtle Manual
BU 0201	Burmese Python
TG 0305	Tokay Geckos
CS 0401	Corn Snakes
RG 0010	Rough Green Snakes
UX 0011	Uromastyx
MS 0405	Milk Snakes
KS 0406	Kingsnakes
RP 0407	Reptile Parasites
DG 0408	Day Geckos
LK 0411	Lizard Keeper's Handbook
DV 0413	Desert Vivaria
WS 0414	What's Wrong With My Snake?
PA 0501S	Pythons of the World, Australia (soft)
PA 0501H	Pythons of the World, Australia (hard)